PREDATOR SHOWDOWN

30 UNBELIEVABLY AWESOME PREDATOR VS. PREDATOR FACE-OFFS!

BY LEE MARTIN

SCHOLASTIC

an imprint of
SCHOLASTIC
www.scholastic.com

Published by Tangerine Press, an imprint of Scholastic Inc.,
557 Broadway, New York, NY 10012
Scholastic Canada Ltd., Markham, Ontario
Scholastic Australia Pty. Ltd, Gosford NSW
Scholastic New Zealand Ltd., Greenmount, Auckland

Produced by becker&mayer!
11120 NE 33rd Place, Suite 101
Bellevue, WA 98004
www.beckermayer.com

becker&mayer!
BOOK PRODUCERS

If you have questions or comments about this book, please visit www.beckermayer.com/customerservice and click on Customer Service Request Form.

Edited by Ben Grossblatt
Designed by Rosanna Brockley
Design assistance by Cortny Helmick
Production management by Jennifer Marx
Image research by Zena Chew and Katie del Rosario

TP4238-1 05/11
Printed in USA
10 9 8 7 6 5 4 3
ISBN: 978-0-545-32071-9
11792
Complies with CPSIA

Predators are hunters. Some silently stalk their prey from the shadows. Some attack in a fury of claws and fangs. Predators prowl their territory relentlessly pursuing their prey, or lie in wait to ambush. But they all must kill to survive. Usually, predators have no reason to fight each other, but what would happen if they did?

3

GRIZZLY (VS.) MOUNTAIN LION

Two top predators—one brawny and the other sleek—go head-to-head. The mountain lion stalks and ambushes, and the grizzly relies on its powerful forearms and formidable claws to grab and slash.

One of the largest mammals in North America, a grizzly standing 7 feet (2.1 m) tall is an imposing sight. Unlike black bears, grizzlies have a hump of muscle on their shoulders and claws as long as human fingers, which they use when digging for roots, climbing trees, clutching their prey, or fighting off foes. However, their bulky size doesn't keep them from reaching speeds of 35 mph (56 kph). Their massive legs and shoulders make them good swimmers.

STATS

SPEED	STRENGTH	BRAINS	ATTACK	DEFENSE
7 / 8	9 / 6	5 / 8	7 / 8	8 / 7

THE SHOWDOWN

An ambush hunter, the mountain lion stalks the grizzly and pounces on it from above. The heavily muscled shoulders of the grizzly prevent the mountain lion from getting a good grip on the back of its neck. The grizzly twists around. It uses its forelegs and claws to get hold of the mountain lion. The grizzly bites, then shakes its massive head to tear the wound.

Strong, stealthy, and graceful, the mountain lion (also known as cougar, panther, and puma) has adapted amazingly well to the civilization that has encroached on its range. It still thrives throughout most of its traditional range in South, Central, and North America. Its legs are designed for quick acceleration and pouncing and its sharp teeth for snatching and tearing prey. The mountain lion stalks and leaps, often from above, clutching the prey with its paws and biting the back of its neck to crush it.

GRIZZLY

MOUNTAIN LION

SCIENTIFIC NAME	URSUS ARCTOS HORRIBILIS	PUMA CONCOLOR
TYPICAL LENGTH (WITHOUT TAIL)	5–8 feet (1.5–2.5 m)	3.25–5.25 feet (1–1.6 m)
SAMPLE PREY	Salmon, moose	Deer, coyotes, porcupines, raccoons
PREDATOR STYLE	Opportunistic; feeds on almost any animal that comes its way	Stalks, pounces; fatal bite to back of the neck; hides kill and returns to eat for several days
RANGE	Northern North America	Canada, much of the United States, and Central and South America

WHO WINS? SEE PAGE 64.

SALTWATER CROCODILE VS. GREAT WHITE SHARK

Both of these mighty predators—one a fish and one a reptile—are excellent swimmers equipped with powerful jaws and sharp teeth. The shark is twice as heavy as the crocodile, but the crocodile is heavily armored.

Saltwater crocodiles, also called salties, are the largest of all crocodiles—some have grown to 23 feet (7 m) long, weighing more than a ton (907 kg)! They are known as good swimmers and ferocious predators. A saltie will lurk at the water's edge, just beneath the surface. When its unsuspecting prey comes close, the croc uses the force of its huge tail to explode from the water. It grabs the animal and drags it underwater. It then holds the victim under until it drowns.

STATS

	SPEED	STRENGTH	BRAINS	ATTACK	DEFENSE
Crocodile	5	8	4	8	8
Shark	8	8	5	10	6

THE SHOWDOWN

The shark senses possible prey and bumps the saltwater crocodile to see if it might be food. The croc, accustomed to defending its territory, attacks, getting its jaws on the shark's fin and going into a death roll. But the crocodile must come up to the surface to breathe, and that's when the shark seizes the opportunity to assault the saltie from below, tearing a huge bite from its exposed soft underbelly.

The largest predatory shark on Earth, with a streamlined, torpedo-like shape and a muscular tail, a great white shark can swim for short bursts at up to 15 mph (24 Kph). Great whites sometimes shoot completely out of the water in pursuit of prey. Their jaws are equipped with as many as 300 triangular, serrated teeth arranged in rows so that when teeth are broken or worn, they are quickly replaced. Sharks use these razor-sharp teeth, which can be up to 3 inches (7.6 cm) long, to rip into their prey and tear off chunks.

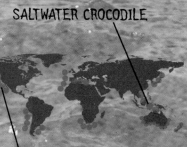

SALTWATER CROCODILE

GREAT WHITE SHARK

	SALTWATER CROCODILE	GREAT WHITE SHARK
SCIENTIFIC NAME	CROCODYLUS POROSUS	CARCHARODON CARCHARIAS
TYPICAL LENGTH	17 feet (5 m)	15–20 feet (4.6–6 m)
SAMPLE PREY	Water buffalo, monkeys, wild boar, sharks	Sea lions, seals, sea turtles, small whales
PREDATOR STYLE	Lurks beneath the surface of the water; leaps and grasps prey, dragging it underwater and holding it until it drowns	Prowls; senses electrical discharges from prey; uses short bursts of speed to attack with vicious bites
RANGE	Southeast Asia to northern Australia	Cool coastal waters around the world

WHO WINS? SEE PAGE 64.

Scorpions have lived on Earth for more than 400 million years. Some species of tarantula feast on animals as large as birds and mice. What happens when the armored survivor meets the fearless fighter?

A small arachnid, the scorpion has a scary set of claws and a curved tail with a venomous stinger. The smaller the scorpion, the stronger its venom—some scorpions' venom is strong enough to kill a human. Scorpions use sensitive hairs on their claws to detect prey nearby. They then either crush the prey or inject it with venom. Digestive juices liquefy the victim so the scorpion can suck up its juices.

STATS*

*The stats for small animals like these should be compared only with the stats of other small animals.

	SPEED	STRENGTH	BRAINS	ATTACK	DEFENSE
Scorpion	8	7	2	8	8
Tarantula	8	7	2	7	5

THE SHOWDOWN

Two scenarios. One: In the dark of night, the scorpion lies in wait. The tarantula is on the prowl for food. Sensing movement, the scorpion grabs with its powerful claws and subdues the spider with venom. Two: The tarantula sets its trap, waiting in its burrow below. The scorpion stumbles in and becomes a quick meal for the tarantula.

For spiders, tarantulas are enormous. They don't build webs but instead set traps to capture their prey, or they hunt at night by sneaking up and attacking. Tarantulas paralyze their prey with venom. Digestive juices turn the victim into a soupy meal. When threatened, a tarantula uses its hind legs to scrape tiny hairs from its belly, sending them flying back toward the threat. The hairs sting and can cause a nasty rash—or even death if inhaled.

FAT-TAILED SCORPION

HORNED BABOON TARANTULA

SCIENTIFIC NAME	ANDROCTONUS AUSTRALIS	CERATOGYRUS BRACHYCEPHALUS
TYPICAL LENGTH	1.5–4 inches (4–10 cm)	2.5–3 inches (6–7.6 cm)
SAMPLE PREY	Insects, mice, frogs	Insects, mice, small lizards
PREDATOR STYLE	Grabs prey; injects venom	Ambushes; crushes prey or injects with venom
RANGE	Northern Africa and the Middle East	Southern Africa

WHO WINS? SEE PAGE 64.

HONEY BADGER vs. WOLVERINE

Neither of these two feisty animals from the weasel family will back down in a fight. In fact, *The Guinness Book of World Records* named the honey badger the most fearless animal on Earth. And the wolverine is known for harassing bears, mountain lions, and wolves!

This fierce creature, no bigger than a medium-sized dog, will attack any animal and has been known to steal a lion's kill. Equipped with long claws, sharp teeth, and loose-fitting skin that allows it to twist away from attackers, the honey badger is both powerful and swift. One was filmed attacking a puff adder snake. Hours after biting into the snake's head and falling unconscious from the potent venom, the honey badger awoke and finished eating the snake.

STATS

	SPEED	STRENGTH	BRAINS	ATTACK	DEFENSE
	7 / 5	6 / 8	6 / 6	7 / 7	6 / 8

THE SHOWDOWN

The aggressive honey badger charges first. The wolverine fights back, leading to a lot of snarling, snapping of jaws, and flying fur. The honey badger's coarse, loose coat renders the wolverine's claws ineffective, and the wolverine's thick fur protects it from the badger's claws and teeth. The honey badger's mouth is not big enough to get a good bite of the wolverine. Finally, the wolverine gets a mouthful of its opponent's leg in its powerful jaws. The wolverine bites down and crushes the leg, seriously wounding the badger.

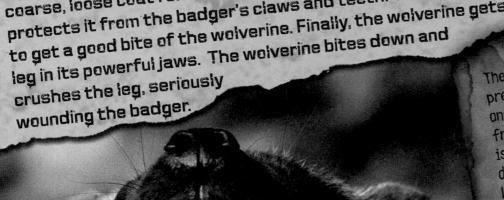

The wolverine is a fearsome predator that will eat almost anything it comes across in the frozen North, where it lives. It is strong and stubborn and will defend its kill against mountain lions, wolves, and grizzly bears. The wolverine's long, dense coat protects it from the cold, and its padded paws and long claws allow it to travel on snow and dig for prey—as well as fight off challengers. Its teeth and jaws are designed for crushing bone and frozen carrion.

WOLVERINE

HONEY BADGER

SCIENTIFIC NAME	MELLIVORA CAPENSIS	GULO GULO
TYPICAL LENGTH (WITHOUT TAIL)	3 feet (91 cm)	2–3 feet (61–91 cm)
SAMPLE PREY	Rodents, termites, snakes and other reptiles	Rodents, rabbits, carrion
PREDATOR STYLE	Tracks and attacks	Ambushes and pounces
RANGE	Greater part of sub-Saharan Africa through the Middle East, to southern Russia, and east to India and Nepal	Northern North America and northern Europe through Asia

WHO WINS? SEE PAGE 64.

KOMODO DRAGON VS. TIGER

Two evenly matched giants that inspire fear and wonder, the world's largest lizard and the world's largest cat face off. They're both ambush hunters, but while tigers rely on their jaws, Komodo dragons count on something even more lethal.

Like crocodiles, Komodo dragons boast powerful bodies, long tails, and sharp teeth. But the dragons have a deadly secret all their own: their bites are almost always fatal. Venom sends prey into shock, and killer bacteria in dragon saliva means prey animals always die of their wounds, even if they escape from an attack. The dragons use their superior sense of smell to scent and track down dying victims from miles away.

STATS

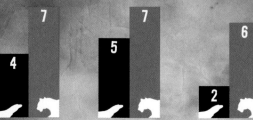

	SPEED	STRENGTH	BRAINS	ATTACK	DEFENSE
	4	5	2	9	4
	7	7	6	8	4

THE SHOWDOWN

Knowing it can outrun its cold-blooded adversary, the tiger makes the first move. With a bounding leap, it pounces on the muscular lizard. The tiger's strategy for defeating large prey is to go right for the throat, which brings the tiger closer to its own doom in the form of the dragon's venomous, poison-filled bite.

Tigers are the undisputed rulers of the Asian jungles they call home. After lying in wait, a charging tiger knocks its prey to the ground and then clamps its crushing jaws to the struggling animal's throat to suffocate it. They are strong enough to jump while carrying dead prey. Tigers can take down hoofed and antlered prey even while swimming. Tigers kill and eat hundreds of humans every year.

TIGER

KOMODO DRAGON

	KOMODO DRAGON	TIGER
SCIENTIFIC NAME	*VARANUS KOMODOENSIS*	*PANTHERA TIGRIS*
TYPICAL LENGTH	10 feet (3 m), including tail	8 feet (2.4 m), including tail
SAMPLE PREY	Deer, boar, water buffalo	Deer, boar, water buffalo
PREDATOR STYLE	Stealth, deadly bite; eats almost all of prey, including hide and hooves	Ambush, power; drags prey to a hidden spot before eating
RANGE	Small islands of Indonesia	India, Southeast Asia, and the Russian Far East

WHO WINS? SEE PAGE 64.

CHINESE PRAYING MANTIS VS. ASIAN GIANT HORNET

Here are two fearsome and savage, but tiny, predators. The Chinese praying mantis is known for its ravenous appetite and cannibalistic behavior. The Asian giant hornet is the world's largest wasp, with a quarter-inch (6 mm) stinger that delivers an attack said to feel like being drilled with a nail.

Swiveling its head from side to side a full 180 degrees (it's the only insect that can do this), the praying mantis surveys its surroundings from its camouflaged perch. Then, almost quicker than the human eye can see, it snags its prey with two front legs. The spiked legs hold the victim, while powerful jaws bite the prey and paralyze it. The praying mantis begins to feed—while its victim is still alive.

STATS*

*The stats for small animals like these should be compared only with the stats of other small animals.

	SPEED	STRENGTH	BRAINS	ATTACK	DEFENSE
Mantis	7	7	5	8	6
Hornet	6	3	5	8 / 8	8

THE SHOWDOWN

The Chinese praying mantis, lying in wait, strikes first. But as soon as it grasps the Asian giant hornet with its spiny forelegs, the hornet uses its mandibles to bite the mantis. When the mantis tries to return the favor, the hornet is close enough to sting the mantis, delivering a toxic load of venom.

This 2-inch (51-mm) killer possesses a stinger, a flesh-eating toxin, and powerful mandibles that can tear the heads off prey. When giant hornets find the nest of their favorite food, the Japanese honeybee, they invade it, raising the temperature so much the bees cannot fight back. The giant hornets then gorge on the bee larvae. These hornets are fast fliers, and their stings are deadly to humans.

CHINESE PRAYING MANTIS

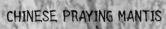

ASIAN GIANT HORNET

SCIENTIFIC NAME	*TENODERA ARIDIFOLIA SINENSIS*	*VESPA MANDARINIA*
TYPICAL LENGTH	4 inches (102 mm)	2 inches (51 mm)
SAMPLE PREY	Insects, caterpillars, tree frogs, small lizards, mice	Honeybees
PREDATOR STYLE	Camouflage, lightning-quick attack	Aggressive hunter
RANGE	Originated in China, but now lives throughout the United States	Temperate and tropical eastern Asia

WHO WINS? SEE PAGE 64.

JACKAL VS. PUFF ADDER

These animals inhabit some of the same areas, so it's likely they would come up against each other. In fact, some jackals specialize in hunting snakes. The puff adder has a great offense and a devastating defense: its long fangs and venomous bite.

On the open savannas and grasslands of Africa, the jackal is an able predator. With its long legs, the jackal can maintain a trotting speed of about 10 mph (16 kph) for a long time. Its long canine teeth are curved, perfect for biting and holding onto prey. Once it gets hold of its victim, the jackal will often shake it like a rag.

STATS

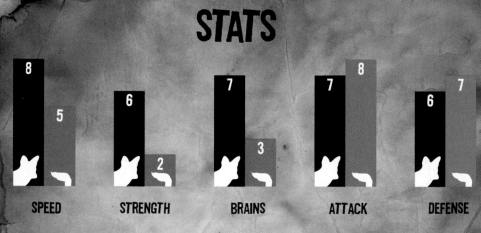

	SPEED	STRENGTH	BRAINS	ATTACK	DEFENSE
Jackal	8	6	7	7	6
Puff Adder	5	2	3	8	7

THE SHOWDOWN

Lying in wait, blending in with its surroundings, the puff adder aims for the element of surprise. It holds itself coiled, the front part of its body in an S-shape, ready to strike when the jackal comes close enough. The jackal, however, has quick reflexes and jumps back when the adder lashes out. The puff adder scores only a glancing blow. The jackal is able to get out of range before the adder reels back to strike again.

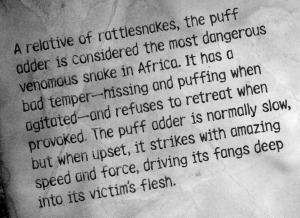

A relative of rattlesnakes, the puff adder is considered the most dangerous venomous snake in Africa. It has a bad temper—hissing and puffing when agitated—and refuses to retreat when provoked. The puff adder is normally slow, but when upset, it strikes with amazing speed and force, driving its fangs deep into its victim's flesh.

GOLDEN JACKAL

PUFF ADDER

SCIENTIFIC NAME	*CANIS AUREUS*	*BITIS ARIENS*
TYPICAL LENGTH	2.5–3 feet (.8–.9 m), not including tail	3.3 feet (1 m)
SAMPLE PREY	Reptiles, rodents, ground-dwelling birds, small antelope	Rodents and other small mammals, birds, lizards
PREDATOR STYLE	Intelligence, resourcefulness	During the day, lies in wait; at dusk, hunts
RANGE	Northern Africa, Europe, Asia	Sub-Saharan Africa

WHO WINS? SEE PAGE 64.

ELECTRIC EEL VS. GREAT BARRACUDA

The electric eel has a uniquely powerful weapon—the ability to stun a large fish like the barracuda with an electrical charge. The barracuda, however, is heftier than an eel, often growing to more than 6 feet (1.8 m) long and weighing 110 pounds (50 kg). This "tiger of the sea" is more than a match for the slippery shocker.

The electric eel is not really an eel but a very long air-breathing fish—some have been known to grow to 8 feet (2.4 m). It produces an electrical charge of 650 volts. That's strong enough to kill a small fish, or stun a human.

STATS

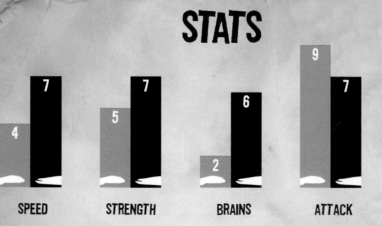

	SPEED	STRENGTH	BRAINS	ATTACK	DEFENSE
Eel	4	5	2	9	4
Barracuda	7	7	6	7	4

THE SHOWDOWN

If the eel catches the barracuda unaware and is able to deliver its electrical charge, it will certainly stun it. But if the barracude can deliver the first blow, it could chomp the eel in half. The barracuda plows through the water to reach the eel. The eel twists around to avoid those toothy jaws and readies its electrical attack.

The toothy underslung jaw and quick speed make the great barracuda one mean predator. A barracuda uses its keen eyesight to locate prey. Then it pursues it at up to 25 mph (40 kph). Its powerful jaws snatch smaller prey whole and are strong enough to bite larger fish in half. Some barracuda have been known to corral prey after eating and hold it captive until they are hungry and ready to eat again.

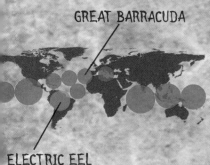

GREAT BARRACUDA

ELECTRIC EEL

SCIENTIFIC NAME	*ELECTROPHORUS ELECTRICUS*	*SPHYRAENA BARRACUDA*
TYPICAL LENGTH	6–8 feet (1.8–2.4 m)	4–5.5 feet (1.2–1.7 m)
SAMPLE PREY	Fish, crab, small mammals	Small fish (can chop large fish in half with its teeth)
PREDATOR STYLE	Searches for prey using electrical signals to navigate in murky water; disables prey with electrical charge	Locates prey by sight, then gives chase
RANGE	Middle and lower Amazon and Orinoco River basins in South America	Most oceans of the world

WHO WINS? SEE PAGE 64.

GRAY WOLF VS. AFRICAN LEOPARD

Here are two beautiful, noble predators. One is canine, the other is feline. One rules the cold lands of North America, the other sub-Saharan Africa. When a top dog goes up against a cat at the top of its predator game, the fur will fly!

The gray wolf is a powerful and intelligent apex predator. Wolves hunt alone, with a pair, or in packs to bring down the large animals they prey on, such as elk. Sometimes, they will set up an ambush to catch their prey. Running at speeds up to 30 mph (48 kph), the wolf separates its prey from the herd and attacks, usually from behind. The wolf's large, sharp teeth are designed to tear at flesh and crush bone. An adult wolf can eat 20 pounds (9 kg) of meat in one sitting.

STATS

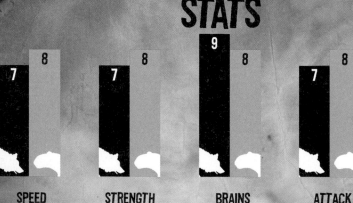

SPEED	STRENGTH	BRAINS	ATTACK	DEFENSE
7 / 8	7 / 8	9 / 8	7 / 8	5 / 7

THE SHOWDOWN

The wolf attempts to get its large canines into one of the leopard's hind legs. The agile leopard twists free and uses its mighty paws to swat at the wolf. The leopard's muscle mass and huge canine teeth spell trouble for the noble gray wolf.

Strong and graceful, this big cat is at home up a tree and on the ground. In fact, it will often drag its kill—perhaps a 200-pound (90.7-kg) antelope—into a tree to keep it safe from scavengers. The leopard has a long body, powerful legs, and a large head. Stealthy and cunning, it will stalk its prey before it pounces and bites the back of the prey's neck, paralyzing it instantly. It then wraps its enormous jaws around the victim's neck to suffocate it.

GRAY WOLF

AFRICAN LEOPARD

SCIENTIFIC NAME	*CANIS LUPUS*	*PANTHERA PARDUS PARDUS*
TYPICAL LENGTH (WITHOUT TAIL)	3–5.25 feet (.9–1.6 m)	4.25–6.25 feet (1.3–1.9 m)
SAMPLE PREY	Moose, elk, rabbits	Antelope, deer, pigs
PREDATOR STYLE	Stalks and pursues	Stalks and pounces
RANGE	Canada and the northern United States	Sub-Saharan Africa

WHO WINS? SEE PAGE 64.

BULL SHARK VS. LEOPARD SEAL

Big teeth, powerful jaws, excellent swimming ability. These two marine predators have it all. Bull sharks are famed for eating almost everything they come across, which has even included dogs, horses, and people. Leopard seals are known for being vicious hunters. Which one will come out on top in a head-to-head fight?

The bull shark is considered by many the shark most likely to attack humans. This is mainly because it swims in shallow coastal waters, but also because of its aggressive and stubborn nature. Named for the wide, blunt shape of its head and the way it butts its prey before attacking, a bull shark will eat whatever it finds. These sharks are able to swim in fresh water and have been found far up the Mississippi River.

STATS

SPEED	STRENGTH	BRAINS	ATTACK	DEFENSE
7 / 8	8 / 8	5 / 6	8 / 6	8 / 6

THE SHOWDOWN

Preferring deeper waters, the leopard seal lures the shark out of the shallows. The leopard seal has speed on its side, but the shark manages to take a bite. The shark's terrible serrated teeth tear a hole in the leopard seal's side. The seal fights back, but its softer body is more vulnerable than the shark's tough skin.

These spotted seals are the most ferocious predators in their home range, the Antarctic. Their sleek bodies make them superb swimmers. They have good senses of both sight and smell underwater. They use their long, sharp teeth to bite and tear at their prey, their favorite being penguins. A leopard seal waits next to an ice shelf for a penguin to dive into the water and then snatches it by its feet. It thrashes the penguin back and forth on the water to skin it before it eats.

BULL SHARK

LEOPARD SEAL

SCIENTIFIC NAME	*CARCHARHINUS LEUCAS*	*HYDRURGA LEPTONYX*
TYPICAL LENGTH	7–11.5 feet (2.1–3.4 m)	10–11.5 feet (3–3.5 m)
SAMPLE PREY	Fish, sharks, rays, turtles	Penguins, seals, fish, squid
PREDATOR STYLE	Hunts in shallow, murky water	Patrols for prey by ice shelf
RANGE	Coastal waters in tropical and subtropical seas around the world	Antarctic waters

WHO WINS? SEE PAGE 64.

RACCOON VS. ORTH AM—RICA RIVER OTTER

These two North American natives are not especially hot-tempered, except when cornered or protecting their young. The otter is in the same family as weasels, known for being fierce fighters. The raccoon's claws are sharp, and it is a good climber and agile mover. Also, the raccoon is smart, similar in intelligence to a chimp.

The bandit-masked raccoon prefers to live in forested areas, but—mainly because it will eat anything, even garbage—it has adapted to live in almost any environment, including cities. Raccoons use their dexterous paws (they look like little hands!) to gather food and catch their prey: bird eggs, snails, mice, and fish, among other things. Their hands are amazingly sensitive, with thousands of nerve endings that they use to learn about what they touch. Raccoons are not particularly aggressive, but if you corner one, watch out!

STATS

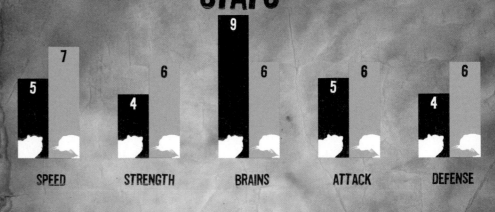

SPEED	STRENGTH	BRAINS	ATTACK	DEFENSE
5 / 7	4 / 6	9 / 6	5 / 6	4 / 6

THE SHOWDOWN

On the banks of a river, the raccoon circles the river otter warily, measuring its adversary. It darts in and bites one of the otter's hind legs. The otter would prefer to fight in the water, so it rolls and pushes the raccoon into the river. Here, the otter can move more quickly. It turns in one fluid motion and clamps its sharp canines on the raccoon's leg, breaking it.

The sleek and playful river otter is built for swimming, with a long, streamlined body, strong tail, and webbed feet. Its agile antics in the water and on land, such as sliding down icy slopes or muddy riverbanks, help it practice hunting and survival skills. Otters can stay underwater for up to eight minutes and can dive up to 60 feet (18.3 m) in search of prey.

RIVER OTTER

RACCOON

SCIENTIFIC NAME	PROCYON LOTOR	LUTRA CANADENSIS
TYPICAL LENGTH (WITHOUT TAIL)	24–37 inches (61–94 cm)	22–31 inches (56–79 cm)
SAMPLE PREY	Crayfish, frogs, mice, insects	Crayfish, frogs, turtles, fish
PREDATOR STYLE	Opportunistic; eats almost anything	Opportunistic; takes advantage of what's available
RANGE	North America, south of Hudson Bay	Canada and parts of the United States as far south as Florida

WHO WINS? SEE PAGE 64.

GOLDEN EAGLE VS. GREAT HORNED OWL

The golden eagle and the great horned owl are two noble, evenly matched raptors. Both have huge wingspans and viselike talons. Both can kill prey far larger and heavier than themselves.

One of the largest birds of prey in North America, the golden eagle can kill prey as large as a deer. Its broad wings span more than 7 feet (2.1 m). Able to dive at speeds of up to 150 mph (240 kph), it snatches up rabbits and other small mammals with its sharp talons. Its large hooked beak efficiently tears the prey's meat from its bones.

STATS

	SPEED	STRENGTH	BRAINS	ATTACK	DEFENSE
Golden Eagle	9	8	4	7	7
Great Horned Owl	6	8	4	8	7

THE SHOWDOWN

The great horned owl perches, turning its head almost completely around as it watches from on high. When it spots the eagle, the owl swoops down silently and attempts to grab it with its talons. The eagle uses its speed to dive out of the way. The eagle flies up and comes at the owl with its talons outstretched. Both birds grapple in a great midair tussle. Feathers fly. The eagle's greater size could give it an advantage over the owl.

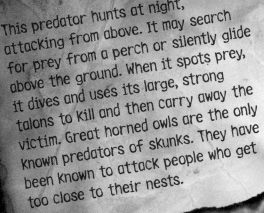

This predator hunts at night, attacking from above. It may search for prey from a perch or silently glide above the ground. When it spots prey, it dives and uses its large, strong talons to kill and then carry away the victim. Great horned owls are the only known predators of skunks. They have been known to attack people who get too close to their nests.

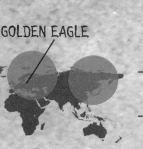

GOLDEN EAGLE

GREAT HORNED OWL

SCIENTIFIC NAME	*AQUILA CHRYSAETOS*	*BUBO VIRGINIANUS*
TYPICAL SIZE	Body: 33–38 inches (84–97 cm) Wingspan: 7.5 feet (2.3 m)	Body: 18–25 inches (46–63 cm) Wingspan: 3.3–4.8 feet (1–1.5 m)
SAMPLE PREY	Rabbits, squirrels, prairie dogs	Rabbits, mice, geese, other raptors
PREDATOR STYLE	Flies low to surprise prey	Nighttime hunter; swoops to attack
RANGE	Throughout the northern hemisphere	Common in North and South America

WHO WINS? SEE PAGE 64.

OCTOPUS **VS.**

Both of these predators have eight legs. The crab has the added advantage of powerful claws at the end of two of its legs. But the octopus is agile, quick, and smart.

When this diminutive predator is alarmed, bright blue pulsating rings appear on its legs and body. It bites its prey with a hidden beak, sending deadly, venomous saliva quickly spreading into the bloodstream of its victim. The octopus is intelligent and crafty, able to hide itself in surprising places, from which it can ambush its prey.

STATS*

*The stats for small animals like this octopus should be compared only with the stats of other small animals.

	SPEED	STRENGTH	BRAINS	ATTACK	DEFENSE
Octopus	7	2	7	8	10
Crab	6	6	2	5	6

THE SHOWDOWN

The king crab attacks first, snapping off one of the octopus's arms and then quickly scuttling away to stay clear of its beak. If the giant crab can continue to disarm the octopus, it has a good chance of winning. But octopuses naturally prey on crabs, cracking the shell with their beaks and then sucking out the meat within.

The red king crab is one of the largest crabs in the world. It makes its home in the freezing cold waters of Bristol Bay, near Alaska. It uses its front two claws, called pincers, to grab and crush its prey.

RED KING CRAB

BLUE-RINGED OCTOPUS

SCIENTIFIC NAME	HAPALOCHLAENA MACULOSA	PARALITHODES CAMTSCHATICUS
TYPICAL SIZE	2–4 inches (5–10 cm)	Body: 11 inches (28 cm); Leg span: 6 feet (1.8 m)
SAMPLE PREY	Fish, shellfish	Sea stars, sand dollars, sea urchins, clams
PREDATOR STYLE	Ambushes from behind; wraps prey in its eight arms and bites, injecting venom	Lurks and snatches up prey or walks the sea floor, hunting
RANGE	Coastal Australia	Bering Sea

WHO WINS? SEE PAGE 64.

FISHER **VS.** RED FOX

The fisher is a relative of the weasel and a fierce predator. The fox is cunning, agile, and fast. Both animals have sharp teeth and claws—and they know how to use them.

Fishers don't actually eat fish, but they are one of the few animals that hunts porcupines. The fisher bites and scratches the porcupine's face until the porcupine can no longer fight back. Then the fisher waits for its prey to bleed to death. The fisher is able to stretch out in narrow tunnels to hunt its prey underground. It has retractable claws and is a good tree climber.

STATS

	SPEED	STRENGTH	BRAINS	ATTACK	DEFENSE
Fisher	6	4	5	6	7
Red Fox	7	5	5	5	6

THE SHOWDOWN

The fisher rushes out of the undergrowth, lunging for the fox's throat. The fox is quick and jumps out of the way. The fox snaps at the fisher, nipping its legs. The fisher twists away. But the fox is built for endurance. Eventually it snaps one of the fisher's legs with its sharp teeth. The fisher will not give up.

The red fox uses its keen senses of sight and hearing to track prey such as mice. In fact, a fox can hear a watch ticking up to 40 yards (36.6 m) away! When it hears a mouse rustling, the fox freezes. Then it launches itself into the air and pounces. Sometimes a fox will play with its prey before killing it. With long legs and a slender body, a fox can run at speeds up to 30 mph (48.2 kph).

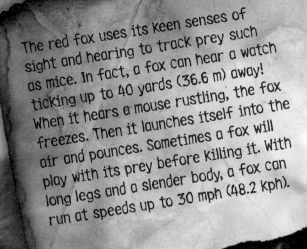

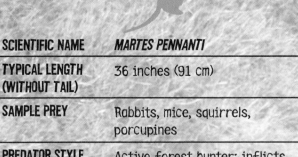

FISHER

RED FOX

SCIENTIFIC NAME	MARTES PENNANTI	VULPES VULPES
TYPICAL LENGTH (WITHOUT TAIL)	36 inches (91 cm)	18–34 inches (46–86 cm)
SAMPLE PREY	Rabbits, mice, squirrels, porcupines	Rabbits, mice, birds, fish, frogs
PREDATOR STYLE	Active forest hunter; inflicts damage with teeth and claws	Solitary, opportunistic hunter; stalks and pounces
RANGE	Northern mountains of North America	North America, northern Africa, Europe, Asia

WHO WINS? SEE PAGE 64.

RED-BELLIED PIRANHA VS. GREEN ANACONDA

Who doesn't know about the piranha's reputation as a ferocious and aggressive carnivore? Stories abound, like the one of a cow that stumbled into a piranha-filled river and was soon reduced to a pile of bones. Still, the green anaconda, the heaviest snake in the world, has nothing to be afraid of. Or does it?

The piranha is known for its razor-sharp teeth (the word *piranha* comes from a word in a Native American language that means "cuts the skin") and its voracious feeding habits. Its powerful jaws have up to 31 interlocking teeth. It doesn't chew but uses its teeth to tear flesh from its prey. Piranhas go out to feed in groups of about 20. When they begin biting, blood fills the water and the piranhas become excited. A feeding frenzy ensues, in which the piranhas strip the prey of all its meat, leaving only bones behind.

STATS

	SPEED	STRENGTH	BRAINS	ATTACK	DEFENSE
🐟	8	2	3	8	6
	5	8	3	6	5

THE SHOWDOWN

The piranha and the anaconda meet in a murky river in the Amazon. The anaconda, realizing it cannot constrict a fish this size, tries to bite the fish, but the fish darts around the snake, tearing chunks from its flesh, until there isn't much snake left to fight.

Though not the longest snake in the world, the anaconda is definitely the heaviest. The anaconda is a constrictor, which means it wraps its massive, muscular body around prey and squeezes. Its jaw is attached with stretchy ligaments that allow it to swallow its prey whole, no matter the size. The anaconda moves slowly on land but is an agile swimmer.

RED-BELLIED PIRANHA

GREEN ANACONDA

SCIENTIFIC NAME	SERRASALMUS NATTERERI	EUNECTES MURINUS
TYPICAL LENGTH	1 foot (.3 m)	20–30 feet (6–9 m)
SAMPLE PREY	Fish, mammals	Wild pigs, deer, birds, turtles
PREDATOR STYLE	Ambushes in groups; feeding-frenzy attack	Lies in wait on land or in water; coils around prey
RANGE	South American rivers	Amazon and Orinoco rain forests

WHO WINS? SEE PAGE 64.

STOAT **VS.** YELLOW MONGOOSE

The stoat and the mongoose look alike, but they are not related. Both are fast and equipped with sharp teeth and claws. Is one more aggressive? If so, that might give it the winning edge.

The stoat, also called the ermine when it has its white winter coat, is a wily, weaselly predator. It has a good sense of smell, which it uses to track its prey. It climbs trees to go after birds and steal their eggs. It can run up to 20 mph (32.1 kph) when chasing prey. Its jaws and sharp teeth kill with a quick bite to the back of the prey's neck.

STATS

SPEED	STRENGTH	BRAINS	ATTACK	DEFENSE
6 / 7	4 / 4	4 / 4	4 / 5	4 / 4

THE SHOWDOWN

The agile mongoose takes a swipe at the stoat and then ducks out of the way. It continues provoking and ducking, somehow avoiding the stoat's strong paws and sharp teeth. Finally, it delivers a crippling bite to the weary stoat's leg.

The mongoose is a famous snake killer. It is quick enough to avoid the snake when it strikes and keeps dodging until the snake is exhausted. Then the mongoose bites the back of the snake's neck, breaking its spine and crushing its head. The mongoose's sharp claws help it dig burrows, scratch for insects, and catch prey.

STOAT

YELLOW MONGOOSE

SCIENTIFIC NAME	*MUSTELA ERMINEA*	*CYNICTIS PENICILLATA*
TYPICAL LENGTH (WITHOUT TAIL)	12 inches (30 cm)	9–13 inches (23–33 cm)
SAMPLE PREY	Mice, insects, rabbits	Snakes, mice, insects, birds
PREDATOR STYLE	Opportunistic; takes whatever it can get its paws on	Quick attack and strong bite
RANGE	UK and northern Europe	Southern Africa

WHO WINS? SEE PAGE 64.

AMERICAN ALLIGATOR VS. NILE CROCODILE

Two colossal beasts with massive jaws, muscular tails, and armored bodies. Both are aggressive and prone to attack when the opportunity presents itself. Although the alligator tends to be heavier, this is a fairly even match-up. Which will have the last bite?

Like their crocodile cousins, alligators look like they're closely related to their dinosaur ancestors. The alligator paddles with its webbed feet, and its powerful tail motors it along. When attacking prey, it uses its tail to lunge out of the water, up to 5 feet (1.5 m) in the air. The alligator swallows smaller prey whole or shears off chunks of meat with its sharp teeth. It also may beat larger prey on the water to break off pieces it can swallow.

STATS

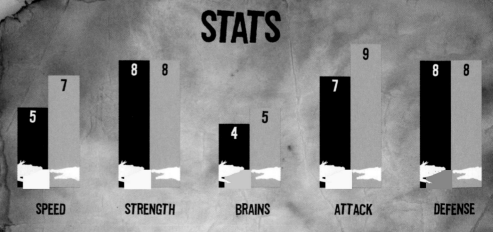

SPEED	STRENGTH	BRAINS	ATTACK	DEFENSE
5 / 7	8 / 8	4 / 5	7 / 9	8 / 8

THE SHOWDOWN

The American alligator and the Nile crocodile swim slowly and warily around each other in the middle of a river. The crocodile snaps at the alligator's leg. The alligator thrashes and opens its terrifying jaws. The gator clamps down on the croc's tail and manages to hang on. But the crocodile is a fierce fighter. It rolls over to hold the alligator underwater. The gator lets go and the croc is able to get in another good snap, with a bite that's among the strongest of any animal on Earth.

The Nile crocodile, a mammoth creature that has changed little in 200 million years, will attack and eat almost anything that comes its way, from fish and turtles in the African rivers and marshes it patrols to an unsuspecting wildebeest or villager at the river's edge. It drags the victim into the water and rolls over to drown it. The crocodile doesn't use those scary-looking teeth to chew but to tear chunks of meat from its prey. Then it tips its head back to swallow the mouthfuls whole.

SCIENTIFIC NAME	*ALLIGATOR MISSISSIPIENSIS*	*CROCODYLUS NILOTICUS*
TYPICAL LENGTH	10–15 feet (3–4.6 m)	16 feet (5 m)
SAMPLE PREY	Fish, birds, snakes, frogs, small mammals	Fish, birds, small hippos, zebras
PREDATOR STYLE	Opportunistic; waits at the water's edge to snatch unwary mammals	Hunts in water; ambushes at water's edge
RANGE	From North Carolina to Rio Grande, Texas	Sub-Saharan Africa

AMERICAN ALLIGATOR

NILE CROCODILE

WHO WINS? SEE PAGE 64.

POLAR BEAR VS. ORCA

The orca, also called the killer whale, is one of the greatest predators in the sea. The polar bear is one of the most impressive predators on land. What will happen when these two tangle?

The polar bear is well adapted to life in the icy Arctic. A thick layer of blubber under its skin keeps it warm and makes it float more easily in water. Thick fur covers its entire body, even its feet, providing traction in the snow. Its paws are webbed and powerful. Polar bears have been seen swimming in open water more than 200 miles (320 km) from land. To catch its main prey, the ringed seal, a polar bear waits for the seal to surface at an open breathing hole. The polar bear may also stalk seals on the ice, slowly crawling to within 20 feet (6.1 m) and then pouncing.

STATS

SPEED	STRENGTH	BRAINS	ATTACK	DEFENSE
4	8	6	8	4
7	9	7	9	4

THE SHOWDOWN

The orca circles the ice floe where a polar bear is resting and nudges it with its snout. The bear uses its strong forepaws to swipe at the orca. It grabs and tears a flipper. Now the orca can't navigate as well. The orca comes up under the polar bear and pushes it into the water. Before long, the bear grows weary, and the orca opens its enormous jaws.

The orca is a dolphin and the largest of its kind. Because of their packlike hunting behavior, these master predators have been called "wolves of the sea." When seals rest on a small ice floe, an orca will use its nose to tip the floe up, while other orcas wait nearby for the seals to slide off into the water. The orca's large jaws are filled with teeth that are up to 4 inches (10 cm) long. It uses its teeth to tear flesh from its prey, but it can swallow a small seal whole.

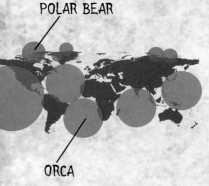

POLAR BEAR

ORCA

SCIENTIFIC NAME	*URSUS MARITIMUS*	*ORCINUS ORCA*
TYPICAL LENGTH	7–8 feet (2.1–2.5 m)	23–32 feet (7–9.7 m)
SAMPLE PREY	Seals	Seals, sea lions, fish
PREDATOR STYLE	Waits at breathing holes; swipes with powerful paws	Hunts in groups (pods)
RANGE	Arctic	Oceans around the world

WHO WINS? SEE PAGE 64.

With their heavy armor and protruding skulls, these two predators resemble their long-ago dinosaur relatives. The alligator snapping turtle boasts quick reflexes and a mean-looking hooked jaw. The caiman has incredible bite force and can move quickly in water.

The largest of the freshwater turtles in North America (and possibly the world), the alligator snapping turtle, with its distinctive ridged shell, looks like a holdover from the time of the dinosaurs. The turtle has a large head with powerful jaws and a hooked beak. It can spend up to 20 minutes underwater as it lures unsuspecting prey close enough to snatch with lightning-quick movements.

STATS

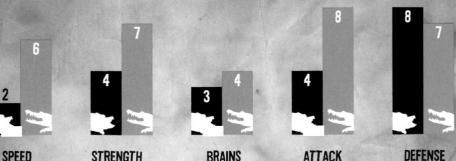

	SPEED	STRENGTH	BRAINS	ATTACK	DEFENSE
Turtle	2	4	3	4	8
Caiman	6	7	4	8	7

THE SHOWDOWN

Camouflaged in the murky riverbed, the alligator snapping turtle waits for its dinner. As the caiman nears, the snapper's head shoots forward, its powerful hooked jaws just missing the croc's vulnerable belly. (Bony plates on the caiman's back protect it from attack.) With a splash, the caiman twists to face its attacker, and its large jaws open to crush the turtle's head.

Caimans are part of the crocodile family, and like crocodiles, they use their muscular tails and webbed feet to propel themselves through the water to hunt for food. A caiman's broad snout holds an impressive set of teeth, which the caiman uses to tear its prey apart. The caiman's heavily armored skin protects it from predators. During the day, the caiman dozes in its burrow. At night, it comes out to patrol the river's edge and use its highly developed senses to find prey.

ALLIGATOR SNAPPING TURTLE

CAIMAN

SCIENTIFIC NAME	MACROCHELYS TEMMINCKII	CAIMAN CROCODILUS
TYPICAL LENGTH	2.2 feet (.7 m)	4–6 feet (1.2–1.8 m)
SAMPLE PREY	Fish, snakes, frogs, other turtles	Fish, turtles, frogs, water birds, wild pigs
PREDATOR STYLE	Deception, ambush; uses a lure (a worm-shaped protrusion on its tongue) and lies in wait to snatch prey	Cruises the water and uses its keen senses to hunt for prey
RANGE	Southern United States	Tropical Central and South America

WHO WINS? SEE PAGE 64.

TASMANIAN DEVIL VS. [DINGO]

The intelligent dingo goes up against the Tasmanian devil, with its reputation for unpredictable behavior. The dingo is an ambush hunter, and the devil is a stalker. The dingo's jaws are bigger, but the Tasmanian devil's jaws exert more force, pound for pound, than those of any other mammal in the world.

The Tasmanian devil is known for impressive displays of ferocity—baring its teeth, lunging, and spine-chilling screeches and growls. In size and shape, these dangerous mammals look a bit like baby bears, but don't let these cuddly bundles of fur fool you; with their oversized heads and strong jaws filled with pointy teeth, Tasmanian devils exert great biting force. They'll eat almost anything they can get their teeth on and will consume their prey completely, including hair and bones.

STATS

	SPEED	STRENGTH	BRAINS	ATTACK	DEFENSE
Tasmanian Devil	5	5	4	7	6
Dingo	8	5	8	5	4

THE SHOWDOWN

The Tasmanian devil patiently lies in wait. When the dingo passes by, the devil ambushes, getting in the first bite and seriously wounding the wild dog. As they struggle, the dingo's agility, strength, and stamina wear the devil down. But the devil's fearsome rage and strong bite take a toll on its foe. Fortunately for the dingo, its large jaws allow it to get a mouthful of the devil.

Independent and intelligent, this member of the dog family uses its smarts to survive in the harsh environment of its native Australia. Dingoes generally hunt for rabbits, rodents, birds, and lizards, but in a pack they can bring down an animal as large and powerful as a kangaroo. The dingo is slightly smaller than a German shepherd and gets high marks for speed, agility, and strength. Like a wolf's, its canine teeth are large and sharp.

DINGO

TASMANIAN DEVIL

SCIENTIFIC NAME	*SARCOPHILUS HARRISII*	*CANIS LUPUS DINGO*
TYPICAL LENGTH (WITHOUT TAIL)	1.7–2.6 feet (.5–.8 m)	3.5–4 feet (1.1–1.2 m)
SAMPLE PREY	Snakes, birds, fish, carrion	Rabbits, birds, rodents, lizards
PREDATOR STYLE	Ambush, power; jaws crush bones and all of prey eaten	Like wolf cousins, the dingo stalks its prey; uses stamina to chase and pounce
RANGE	The island of Tasmania, off Australia	Australia (not Tasmania) and Southeast Asia

WHO WINS? SEE PAGE 64.

RETICULATED PYTHON VS. KING COBRA

The longest snake in the world vs. the largest venomous snake. Each is known for its strength, speed, and cunning. But while the reticulated python has size on its side, the king cobra is known as "the snake eater" for a reason.

Reticulated pythons are constrictors. The python ambushes its prey in a blur of coils, biting to secure its hold and then gradually squeezing until the animal can no longer breathe. It takes only minutes for the python to kill its prey. Then it swallows its food whole. Though they are not venomous, pythons can deliver vicious bites with their sharp, curved teeth—100 in all! Reticulated pythons have been known to attack people.

STATS

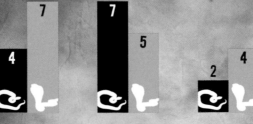

SPEED	STRENGTH	BRAINS	ATTACK	DEFENSE
4 / 7	7 / 5	2 / 4	9 / 7	4 / 5

THE SHOWDOWN

Flicking its tongue, the king cobra collects the information it needs to track its prey. With sharp eyesight, it spots the moving python. When the python slithers within the cobra's strike range, the snake eater strikes. The bite sends venom coursing through the python's body. Using its superior strength, the python coils around the cobra and fights back. But the king cobra's venom is already sapping the python's strength.

Although they don't have the strongest venom, King cobras can deliver enough in a single bite to kill 20 people. King cobras have been found as long as 18 feet (5.5 m). When cornered, the king cobra raises its head and up to one-third of its body straight into the air, unfurling its hood and hissing viciously. King cobras can attack as far as they can raise their bodies; for an adult cobra, this yields a strike zone of up to 5 feet (1.5 m).

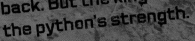

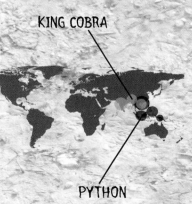

KING COBRA

PYTHON

SCIENTIFIC NAME	*PYTHON RETICULATUS*	*OPHIOPHAGUS HANNAH*
TYPICAL LENGTH	10–20 feet (3–6 m)	13 feet (4 m)
SAMPLE PREY	Rodents, wild boar, deer	Snakes, lizards, small mammals
PREDATOR STYLE	Ambush, constricting coils	Quick attack, venomous bite
RANGE	Southeast Asia and nearby islands	Rain forests and plains of India, southern China, and Southeast Asia

WHO WINS? SEE PAGE 64.

PEREGRINE FALCON VS. BOBCAT

Cat against bird. Usually the cat would win, but the peregrine falcon has the advantage of terrific diving speed, strong talons, and a vicious hooked beak. The bobcat, on the other hand, is quick and agile, and able to leap as far as 10 feet (3 m) to pounce.

The fastest-flying birds in the world, peregrine falcons can reach diving speeds of 200 mph (320 kph). They snag prey in midair with their talons. A bite to the neck kills the victim instantly. Smaller animals, such as bats, may be eaten in flight. Larger prey is taken back to the falcon's perch to be eaten or cached for later.

STATS

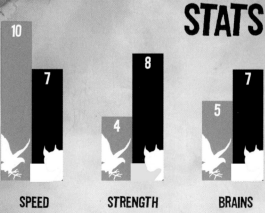

	SPEED	STRENGTH	BRAINS	ATTACK	DEFENSE
Falcon	10	4	5	6	3
Bobcat	7	8	7	7	6

THE SHOWDOWN

Using its airborne advantage to the fullest, the peregrine falcon dives at the bobcat, tearing at the feline with its talons. The bobcat returns the fight with its powerful paws, trying to pull or bat the falcon to the ground. Although the falcon is strong and fast, the size of the bobcat lends it a distinct advantage.

These elusive nocturnal creatures are about twice the size of a house cat. With long legs and large, powerful paws, bobcats are able to leap 10 feet (3 m) to pounce on prey. The bobcat hunts by stalking prey from under cover and pouncing on it when the prey wanders close. Then the bobcat grabs the animal and delivers a bite to the neck.

PEREGRINE FALCON

BOBCAT

SCIENTIFIC NAME	FALCO PEREGRINUS	LYNX RUFUS
TYPICAL SIZE	Body: 14–19 inches (36–48 cm) Wingspan: 3.5 feet (1 m)	26–41 inches (66–104 cm) long, not including tail
SAMPLE PREY	Starlings, pigeons, bats	Rabbits, birds, mice, squirrels
PREDATOR STYLE	Pursuit; high-speed dive to capture prey	Stealth; leaps and pounces
RANGE	Throughout the world, except Antarctica	Southern Canada, United States, and northern Mexico

WHO WINS? SEE PAGE 64.

BULLET ANT VS. ASSASSIN BUG

These two predators have fierce stings, and they're not afraid to use them. The assassin bug is an ambush hunter, while the bullet ant goes out in search of prey. The question: Which insect would strike first?

This tiny predator is named for its painful sting. (Some say it feels like being shot.) Although they are not particularly aggressive, bullet ants will attack if their nest is threatened. The ants swarm out, releasing a stinky smell and making a shrill, scratchy sound by rubbing body parts together. Then they grab the intruders and impale them on their retractable stingers.

STATS*

*The stats for small animals like these should be compared only with the stats of other small animals.

	SPEED	STRENGTH	BRAINS	ATTACK	DEFENSE
Bullet Ant	8	9	5	7	7
Assassin Bug	8	5	3	8	5

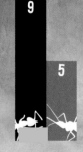
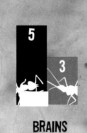
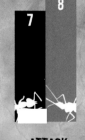
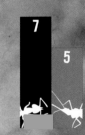

THE SHOWDOWN

The assassin bug catches the bullet ant by surprise. Attempting to disable its attacker, the ant tears at the assassin bug's legs with its mandibles. The ant's stinger is located on its abdomen, so it must engage in close combat to inject the assassin bug with venom. With all its strength, the ant pulls its stealthy attacker into its clutches.

Assassin bugs are called that because they are masters of the surprise attack. They lie in wait for their prey, quickly stab the victim, and then inject it with lethal venom. The venom liquefies the victim's tissues, so the assassin bug can suck up the juice through its long beak. These bugs are aggressive and not afraid to attack prey much larger than themselves. When food becomes scarce, they will go out to hunt for prey.

ASSASSIN BUG

BULLET ANT

	PARAPONERA CLAVATA	RASAHUS HAMATUS
SCIENTIFIC NAME	PARAPONERA CLAVATA	RASAHUS HAMATUS
TYPICAL LENGTH	1 inch (2.5 cm)	1 inch (2.5 cm)
SAMPLE PREY	Termites and other insects	Caterpillars and other insects, small mammals
PREDATOR STYLE	Patrols and attacks	Stalks and strikes
RANGE	Central and South America	Varieties throughout the world

WHO WINS? SEE PAGE 64.

LION VS. SPOTTED HYENA

Lions and hyenas are sworn enemies. Male lions routinely steal hyenas' kill. Hyenas chase female lions and steal their kill. Hyenas also kill and eat sick or injured lions. But when the two face off, which will come out on top—the king of the beasts or the maniacal laughing hyena?

The second-largest felines (only tigers are bigger), lions are apex predators of the savannas. Lions chase away intruders with intimidating roars. They have powerful legs and canine teeth that are 3 inches (8 cm) long. Lions are stealthy, sneaking up on their prey and then attacking with a rush and a leap. They kill larger animals with a bite to the neck or head, but they can take care of smaller animals with a simple swipe of a paw.

STATS

	SPEED	STRENGTH	BRAINS	ATTACK	DEFENSE
	4 / 7	5 / 7	8 / 6	8 / 7	4 / 4

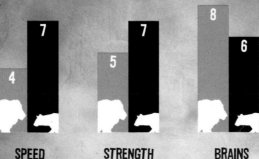

THE SHOWDOWN

Hyenas can run faster for longer distances, but it would require a pack of them to take down a lion—and this hyena is hunting alone. The lion hides in the tall grasses, stalking the hyena until it is close enough for a power rush and attack. Snarling and snapping, the hyena mounts a counterattack, but the lion's massive jaws and major canines just might be unstoppable.

These skillful hunters use their strong jaws to chomp through skin and bone. Although they can hang onto a moving animal with their jaws, they do not have a killing bite. Hyenas are fast and can run long distances. They chase a prey animal to its death, attack it, and tear chunks out of it until it dies. Bold and dangerous, hyenas have been known to attack humans.

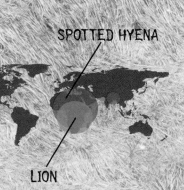

SPOTTED HYENA

LION

SCIENTIFIC NAME	PANTHERA LEO	CROCUTA CROCUTA
TYPICAL LENGTH (WITHOUT TAIL)	4.5–6.5 feet (1.4–2 m)	3–5 feet (.9–1.5 m)
SAMPLE PREY	Wildebeest, impala, zebra, buffalo	Wildebeest and zebra are favorites, but will scavenge anything
PREDATOR STYLE	Stalks, rushes; strangles victims with bite to the neck	Persistence; runs prey to exhaustion
RANGE	Sub-Saharan Africa; Gir Forest in India	Throughout much of Africa, the Arabian Peninsula, and India

WHO WINS? SEE PAGE 64.

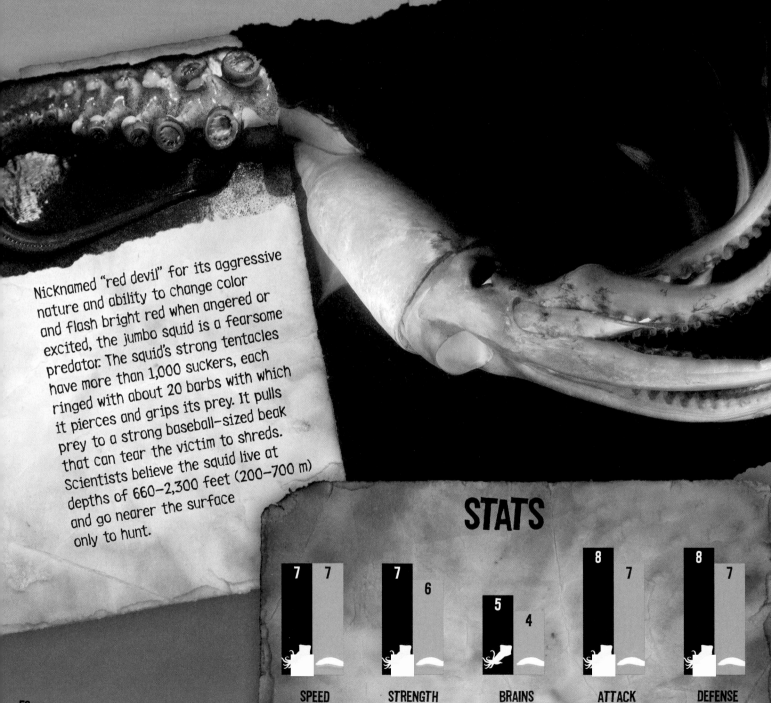

JUMBO SQUID VS. GIANT MORAY EEL

The notoriously aggressive jumbo squid is armed with eight tentacles lined with sharp suction cups. The giant moray, the largest of the moray eels, is equipped with large strong jaws and long canine teeth.

Nicknamed "red devil" for its aggressive nature and ability to change color and flash bright red when angered or excited, the jumbo squid is a fearsome predator. The squid's strong tentacles have more than 1,000 suckers, each ringed with about 20 barbs with which it pierces and grips its prey. It pulls prey to a strong baseball-sized beak that can tear the victim to shreds. Scientists believe the squid live at depths of 660–2,300 feet (200–700 m) and go nearer the surface only to hunt.

STATS

	SPEED	STRENGTH	BRAINS	ATTACK	DEFENSE
	7 / 7	7 / 6	5 / 4	8 / 7	8 / 7

THE SHOWDOWN

The giant moray waits in a dark crevice. When the squid glides by, the eel darts out, its powerful jaws wide-open. It is able to grasp only a tip of one of the squid's tentacles, however, before the squid jets away, spraying ink behind it. When the squid circles again, it attempts to wrap its tentacles around the eel. But the eel manages to bite into the squid's soft body, inflicting serious injury.

This snakelike fish lives in the crevices of coral reefs, waiting for unsuspecting prey to swim by. The eel's skin is camouflaged and covered with mucus to protect it as it swims swiftly by the sharp edges of the reef. Its strong jaws are lined with pointy teeth. Even the inside of its mouth is camouflaged—it must keep its mouth open at all times so water can circulate through its gills. The eel's eyesight is not good, so it relies on its keen sense of smell to find prey.

SCIENTIFIC NAME	*DOSIDICUS GIGAS*	*GYMNOTHORAX JAVANICUS*
TYPICAL LENGTH	6 feet (1.8 m), including tentacles	10 feet (3 m)
SAMPLE PREY	Lanternfish, shrimp, mollusks, other squid	Fish, octopus, other eels
PREDATOR STYLE	Uses barbed suckers on tentacles to grasp and drag prey to mouth	Sniffs out prey, then ambushes and bites
RANGE	Warmer waters of the Pacific Ocean and the coast of Alaska	Indo-Pacific region

JUMBO SQUID

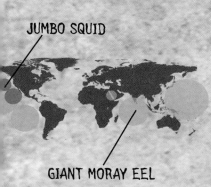

GIANT MORAY EEL

WHO WINS? SEE PAGE 64.

RABID WOLF SPIDER VS. BLACK WIDOW

Two small but creepy predators battle it out. The wolf spider is an ambush hunter, lying in wait for prey and then running out to attack. The black widow traps prey in its web and then administers a lethal bite.

This spider gets its name because of its wolflike hunting strategy: it stalks its prey, then charges in to attack. Also, it is not afraid to assault a creature much larger than itself. The wolf spider does not build a web, but instead moves slowly or waits quietly for its prey, tracking it by watching and feeling its movements through vibrations in the ground. After the wolf spider subdues its victim, it sucks its insides out.

STATS*

*The stats for small animals like these should be compared only with the stats of other small animals.

	SPEED	STRENGTH	BRAINS	ATTACK	DEFENSE
Rabid Wolf Spider	5	5	3	8	6
Black Widow	5	4	2	6	8

THE SHOWDOWN

The rabid wolf spider charges the black widow as it sits in its web, poking at it with its two front legs. But the black widow moves quickly and menacingly, and the wolf spider retreats. Unable to resist, the wolf spider attacks again. The wolf spider is larger than the black widow, but the black widow is quick and the venom in its bite packs a punch.

The black widow is the most venomous spider in North America, but it is more dangerous to other bugs than it is to humans. The glossy black spider with the bright red or orange hourglass shape on its abdomen builds a messy but very strong and sticky web to catch its prey. When the black widow senses prey in its web, it comes out of hiding, bites the victim, injects venom, and holds it with its legs until it stops struggling. Then the spider carries its prize back to its hiding place to suck out its juices.

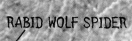

RABID WOLF SPIDER

BLACK WIDOW

	RABIDOSA RABIDA	LATRODECTUS MACTANS
SCIENTIFIC NAME	*RABIDOSA RABIDA*	*LATRODECTUS MACTANS*
TYPICAL LENGTH (WITHOUT LEGS)	Female: 1 inch (2.5 cm)	Female: .5 inch (1.3 cm)
SAMPLE PREY	Insects	Insects
PREDATOR STYLE	Stalks and chases prey	Attacks insects caught in web
RANGE	Central and eastern North America	Throughout much of the United States and southern Canada

WHO WINS? SEE PAGE 64.

OSPREY VS. ~~BALD EAGLE~~

These two birds of prey inhabit many of the same regions and occasionally fight over prey. The bald eagle is definitely bigger, but the osprey is a faster flier and is more agile in the air.

From as high as 100 feet (30 m) in the sky, the osprey sees a fish and dives toward the water. It grips the fish with its claws and pulls it from the water. The osprey has to be powerful to drag a big, slippery fish to the surface, shake the water from its wings, and then bring it back to the nest.

STATS

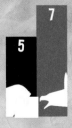

SPEED	STRENGTH	BRAINS	ATTACK	DEFENSE
8 7	6 7	5 5	5 7	4 6

THE SHOWDOWN

Swooping down upon the osprey, the eagle attacks from above. The osprey fights back, struggling to sink its talons into the eagle. The size and weight of the eagle, as well as its formidable beak, give it an advantage. Can the osprey's speed balance the scales?

The bald eagle has a distinctive white head and tail, a large brown body, and a bright yellow hooked beak. It holds its wings out flat as it soars overhead in large looping circles and uses its sharp eyes to watch for prey. When it sees prey, it swoops down and uses sharp talons to grab its victim. Its strong beak tears at the meat.

OSPREY

BALD EAGLE

SCIENTIFIC NAME	*PANDION HALIAETUS*	*HALIAEETUS LEUCOCEPHALUS*
TYPICAL SIZE	Body: 22 inches (56 cm) Wingspan: 60–70 inches (152–178 cm)	Body: 32 inches (81 cm) Wingspan: 80 inches (203 cm)
SAMPLE PREY	Fish	Fish, large birds, mammals
PREDATOR STYLE	Hovers over water, then dives to snatch prey	Swoops down to grab fish from stream or bay; will steal other animals' kills
RANGE	Throughout North America, especially Alaska and Canada	North America

WHO WINS? SEE PAGE 64.

SERVAL VS. CHEETAH

The serval and the cheetah are great hunters of the African savannas. The serval is the most successful hunter of the cat family because of its sharp sense of hearing and ability to pounce and catch animals on the ground and in the air. The cheetah is strong and agile; it uses its tail as a rudder to help it turn midsprint.

The serval, an African native, is a long-legged, medium-sized cat with huge ears. It uses its excellent hearing to locate prey—it can even hear animals in their burrows underground. When the serval finds an animal, it leaps high into the air and pounces with enough force to stun the prey. It holds the victim down with a paw and breaks its spine with a bite to the neck. The serval is able to leap 9 feet (2.7 m) into the air and catch birds in flight.

STATS

	SPEED	STRENGTH	BRAINS	ATTACK	DEFENSE
	7 / 9	6 / 7	7 / 7	8 / 7	6 / 7

THE SHOWDOWN

The serval and the cheetah stalk each other in the tall grass. Each is silent and well camouflaged. Suddenly, the serval leaps out of the grass and onto the cheetah's back. The cheetah hisses and twists onto the ground, forcing the serval off. The cheetah lunges at the serval, whacking at it with powerful paws. The serval tries to leap again, but the cheetah uses its weight and strength to hold the serval down with its paws.

Built for speed, the cheetah's full-out stride when sprinting after prey is about 20 feet (6 m)—the same as that of a racehorse. But a cheetah can run much faster than a racehorse, up to 70 mph (112 kph) over short distances. When the cheetah catches its prey, it holds it by the neck to strangle it. The cheetah pants and catches its breath before carrying the prey to a safe place to eat.

SERVAL

CHEETAH

	SCIENTIFIC NAME	FELIS SERVAL	ACINONYX JUBATUS
	TYPICAL LENGTH (WITHOUT TAIL)	3 feet (.9 m)	4 feet (1.2 m)
	SAMPLE PREY	Antelope, birds, hares, frogs, fish	Antelope, birds, rabbits
	PREDATOR STYLE	Stalks, leaps, and pounces	Stalks and sprints after prey
	RANGE	Found in most parts of Africa	Central and southern Africa

WHO WINS? SEE PAGE 64.

GREAT HAMMERHEAD SHARK VS. BLUE MARLIN

Two oceanic predators go (weirdly shaped) head-to-head. The shape of a hammerhead's head is a wide, flat *T*, and the blue marlin's head is narrow and sharp. The hammerhead has a mouthful of sharp teeth, while the blue marlin can effectively use its spearlike upper jaw in a battle.

The massive hammerhead uses its bizarrely shaped head to find prey. With eyes located on the ends of the crossbar and sensory organs covering it, the shark is well suited for scanning the ocean and locating prey. The shark sometimes uses its head to pin down its favorite fish, the stingray, biting off chunks until the ray can no longer move. The hammerhead prefers to swim and hunt in warm, shallow waters, which may be part of the reason it is considered dangerous to humans.

STATS

	SPEED	STRENGTH	BRAINS	ATTACK	DEFENSE
	4 / 7	4 / 7	2 / 6	9 / 7	4 / 4

THE SHOWDOWN

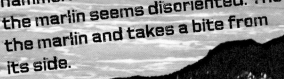

The blue marlin slashes at the hammerhead, provoking it to move into deeper waters. The marlin turns and swims full speed at the hammerhead. The shark veers away and, keeping clear of the marlin's spear, swings around to bite the marlin's tail. The hammerhead catches the marlin's tail and shakes the big fish. When the shark lets go, the marlin seems disoriented. The hammerhead charges the marlin and takes a bite from its side.

Deep blue on top, with a white belly and a sword-shaped upper jaw, the blue marlin is a striking fish. It's large, too—one of the largest fish in the world. It swims in the open waters of the Atlantic Ocean, hunting on the surface for tuna or diving deep for squid. Able to reach high speeds, the marlin uses its spear to slash at schools of fish, stunning them and then gobbling them up.

GREAT HAMMERHEAD SHARK

BLUE MARLIN

SCIENTIFIC NAME	*SPHYMA MOKARRAN*	*MAKAIRA NIGRICANS*
TYPICAL LENGTH	13–20 feet (4–6 m)	Up to 14 feet (4.3 m)
SAMPLE PREY	Sharks, rays, fish, squid	Fish, squid
PREDATOR STYLE	Scans and patrols for prey	Uses "spear" to slash and stun prey
RANGE	Temperate and tropical waters around the world	Temperate and tropical waters of the Atlantic Ocean

WHO WINS? SEE PAGE 64.

JAGUAR VS. BURMESE PYTHON

The jaguar and the python are two stealthy and solitary hunters. Both are good swimmers. Both have big jaws and a mean bite. In a head-to-head battle, which would come out on top?

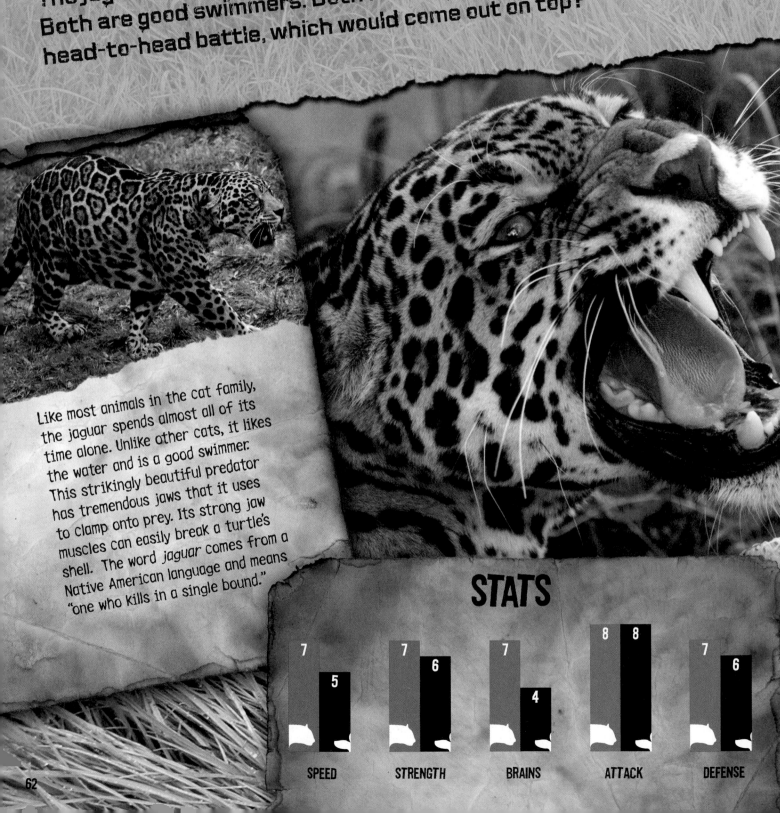

Like most animals in the cat family, the jaguar spends almost all of its time alone. Unlike other cats, it likes the water and is a good swimmer. This strikingly beautiful predator has tremendous jaws that it uses to clamp onto prey. Its strong jaw muscles can easily break a turtle's shell. The word *jaguar* comes from a Native American language and means "one who kills in a single bound."

STATS

	SPEED	STRENGTH	BRAINS	ATTACK	DEFENSE
Jaguar	7	7	7	8	7
Python	5	6	4	8	6

THE SHOWDOWN

Both animals are in the water. The Burmese python bites the jaguar and begins to wrap its huge body around the cat. The cat twists and uses its claws to fight off the python. The jaguar is a very fast swimmer. It gets away and then comes back to clamp its massive jaws on the python's head.

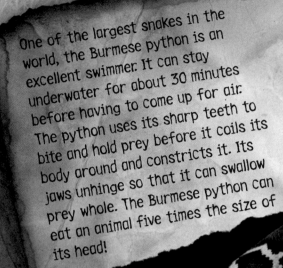

One of the largest snakes in the world, the Burmese python is an excellent swimmer. It can stay underwater for about 30 minutes before having to come up for air. The python uses its sharp teeth to bite and hold prey before it coils its body around and constricts it. Its jaws unhinge so that it can swallow prey whole. The Burmese python can eat an animal five times the size of its head!

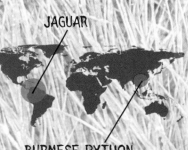

JAGUAR

BURMESE PYTHON

SCIENTIFIC NAME	PANTHERA ONCA	PYTHON MOLURUS BIVITTATUS
TYPICAL LENGTH	5–6 feet (1.5–1.8 m), not including tail	16–23 feet (5–7 m)
SAMPLE PREY	Fish, turtles, caimans, deer	Rabbits, mice, rats, lizards, snakes, birds
PREDATOR STYLE	Ambushes and pounces; kills with a powerful bite	Stalks, bites, and squeezes until prey suffocates
RANGE	Central and South America (mainly Amazon basin)	Southeast Asia

WHO WINS? SEE PAGE 64.

THE WINNERS

p. 4–5:
GRIZZLY VS. MOUNTAIN LION
Winner: Grizzly Bear
The cougar is a top predator, but the grizzly simply overmatches it.

p. 6–7:
SALTWATER CROCODILE VS. GREAT WHITE SHARK
Winner: Saltwater Crocodile
It's an upset! The croc has body armor and a stronger bite than the great white. Also, the croc—which doesn't have to keep swimming to stay alive—is more versatile.

p. 8–9:
FAT-TAILED SCORPION VS. HORNED BABOON TARANTULA
Winner: Fat-Tailed Scorpion
The scorpion can strike faster than the tarantula, and its shell is strong, providing good protection against the tarantula's bite.

p. 10–11:
HONEY BADGER VS. WOLVERINE
Winner: Wolverine
The honey badger is incredibly aggressive, but the wolverine has a bigger mouth and a stronger bite. The honey badger's smaller mouth and teeth just can't compete with the wolverine's larger weapons.

p. 12–13:
KOMODO DRAGON VS. TIGER
Winner: Tie
The tiger is much stronger and more agile than the dragon, but one bite from the dragon could spell doom for the tiger. The tiger kills the dragon, but it dies days later from an infected bite.

p. 14–15:
CHINESE PRAYING MANTIS VS. ASIAN GIANT HORNET
Winner: Asian Giant Hornet
The praying mantis is a great hunter, but before it could deliver a killing bite to its opponent's head, the hornet's sting would paralyze it.

p. 16–17:
GOLDEN JACKAL VS. PUFF ADDER
Winner: Puff Adder
This is a tough battle between two tough predators. Although the jackal is used to hunting and eating snakes, it can't handle the adder's deadly venom.

p. 18–19:
ELECTRIC EEL VS. GREAT BARRACUDA
Winner: Electric Eel
The barracuda will never get a chance to use its fantastically sharp teeth. The electric eel's stunning charge leads to victory before the biting can begin.

p. 20–21:
GRAY WOLF VS. AFRICAN LEOPARD
Winner: African Leopard
The leopard has a bigger bite and larger canine teeth. Unlike the wolf, it can fight with its powerful forepaws.

p. 22–23:
BULL SHARK VS. LEOPARD SEAL
Winner: Bull Shark
The shark is the definite winner because of its bigger, stronger bite. On the defensive side, it has tougher skin than the leopard seal.

p. 24–25:
RACCOON VS. NORTH AMERICAN RIVER OTTER
Winner: North American River Otter
In the water, the otter would definitely win. It's much quicker and more agile there. Also, its mouth is bigger than a raccoon's and would inflict more damage.

p. 26–27:
GOLDEN EAGLE VS. GREAT HORNED OWL
Winner: Golden Eagle
These two raptors are well matched. However, the eagle has the edge because it is bigger and can maneuver better in the air.

p. 28–29:
BLUE-RINGED OCTOPUS VS. RED KING CRAB
Winner: Blue-Ringed Octopus
Even though this is one very big crab and one very small octopus, the crab can't win against the octopus's beak and venom.

p. 30–31:
FISHER VS. RED FOX
Winner: Red Fox
The fisher puts up a good fight, but it can't get past the fox's bigger bite.

p. 32–33:
RED-BELLIED PIRANHA VS. GREEN ANACONDA
Winner: Red-Bellied Piranha
The anaconda is huge, but it's a constrictor and can't squeeze a fish so small. The piranha would beat the snake bite-by-bite.

p. 34–35:
STOAT VS. YELLOW MONGOOSE
Winner: Yellow Mongoose
This would be a tough fight for both animals, but in the end, the mongoose is the more aggressive fighter and would win the match.

p. 36–37:
AMERICAN ALLIGATOR VS. NILE CROCODILE
Winner: Nile Crocodile
In this battle of equals, the croc comes out on top. It's simply a fiercer competitor.

p. 38–39:
POLAR BEAR VS. ORCA
Winner: Orca
There's a reason orcas are called killer whales. And although polar bears are comfortable in the water, they don't have a chance against orcas. Those huge jaws full of long, pointy teeth spell doom for the polar bear.

p. 40–41:
ALLIGATOR SNAPPING TURTLE VS. CAIMAN
Winner: Caiman
This is a close match. Although the snapping turtle has an extremely strong bite, the caiman's bite is strong enough to crack a turtle's shell. The caiman's speed advantage puts it over the top.

p. 42–43:
TASMANIAN DEVIL VS. DINGO
Winner: Tie
The Tasmanian devil has a tremendous bite, but the dingo has size and large canine teeth on its side. The devil is tenacious, and the dingo would suffer a lot of damage. In the end, these two, this time, part ways with neither one claiming victory.

p. 44–45:
RETICULATED PYTHON VS. KING COBRA
Winner: King Cobra
The python is a constrictor, and it usually hunts mammals. It would be harder for it to constrict a snake. The cobra, however, specializes in killing other snakes. With its quick strike, long fangs, and extremely strong venom, it would be the winner in this face-off.

p. 46–47:
PEREGRINE FALCON VS. BOBCAT
Winner: Bobcat
The falcon is strong and fast, and it might be able to injure the bobcat, but the bobcat has greater size, powerful paws, and sharp teeth.

p. 48–49:
BULLET ANT VS. ASSASSIN BUG
Winner: Bullet Ant
The ant's venomous sting gives it the edge in this fight.

p. 50–51:
LION VS. SPOTTED HYENA
Winner: Lion
The lion is known as the King of the beasts for a reason. Even against the hyena's superior speed and strength, the lion's powerful attack means triumph for the cat.

p. 52–53:
JUMBO SQUID VS. GIANT MORAY EEL
Winner: Jumbo Squid
The squid overpowers the eel with its tentacles, and its beak does the rest.

p. 54–55:
RABID WOLF SPIDER VS. BLACK WIDOW
Winner: Rabid Wolf Spider
The black widow's venom is no match for the wolf spider's bite.

p. 56–57:
OSPREY VS. BALD EAGLE
Winner: Bald Eagle
These animals are very evenly matched. However, eagles are known to pester osprey and steal fish from them. With its size and weight advantage, the bald eagle takes the win.

p. 58–59:
SERVAL VS. CHEETAH
Winner: Cheetah
The relatively small-boned cat is bigger and more powerful. Not even the serval's amazing leaps can save it.

p. 60–61:
GREAT HAMMERHEAD SHARK VS. BLUE MARLIN
Winner: Great Hammerhead
The marlin is a worthy opponent that could definitely inflict serious damage, but the larger hammerhead swims away with a win.

p. 62–63:
JAGUAR VS. BURMESE PYTHON
Winner: Jaguar
Jaguars are good at hunting snakes, pythons in particular. The cat's powerful jaws could easily crush the snake's skull.